EXOTIC PETS

21 ANIMALS YOU DIDN'T KNOW YOU CAN ADOPT AS A PET

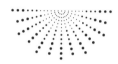

JOHN NEWBORNE

CONTENTS

17 Cutest Baby Animals you wouldn't believe...

This booklet includes:

- 17 OF THE MOST ADORABLE BABY ANIMALS THAT WILL BRING A SMILE TO YOUR FACE
- SURPRISING FUN FACTS ABOUT THESE ANIMALS THAT YOU NEVER KNEW

Get this free booklet and share the fun with these adorable animals that will make your day!

To receive your free _Cutest Baby Animals_ booklet, click the link or scan the QR code below:

https://purelypublishing.activehosted.com/f/7

INTRODUCTION

Weighing in at 200 pounds, Leonardo Di Caprio's $400 African Spurred Tortoise is 20 years old. Honky and Tonky, the names of Reese Witherspoon's miniature donkeys, are now Instagram famous. And of course, Tori Spelling, who not only has a family pig but also takes to bed with her every night, Coco Chanel, her white chicken.

Just a few, among many examples of exotic pets that people legally adopt in the United States. Whether you are an exotic animal enthusiast or just someone who wants to take on the challenge of caring for one of the fascinating undomesticated creatures that inhabit our planet, adopting an exotic pet can be a very exciting and life(style)-changing experience.

If you are anything like me, you love all animals, and whether you have had one or many pets, you are absolutely fascinated with the bond a human can share with another species. I grew up on a farm, surrounded by various animals from all walks of life, each with their own personalities and needs, and let me tell you, when you are around these animals all day, you begin to grow very attached to each one in a different way. Duchess, was the name of my white stallion growing up. She was my best friend and was the beginning of my obsession with exotic pets.

I love me a playful pup and a regal cat as a pet, and they are among the many animals that have been domesticated over hundreds of years to coexist with humans, and are relatively easy pets to care for. But there is something magical about walking down the street with "Abu," my pet capuchin monkey, on my shoulder. He has been a part of the family for five years now. And oh, boy! - he is a handful; it's like having a permanent toddler. He was a rescue who was stripped away from his family at a very young age in the wild. We gave him a loving home, and he has quickly grown to be a family member. You begin to adapt, acclimate, and coexist with a wild species, and you realize it has its own personality, likes and dislikes, and daily routine.

In this book, I will take you through the many exotic animals that can become your roommate and bring a special joy into your life. Some come with more responsibilities and obstacles, while others might not even be legal in your area.

Let's dive into the 21 exotic animals that you can call pets in the United States.

SUGAR GLIDER

THESE CUTE CRITTERS ORIGINATE IN AUSTRALIA. They belong to the marsupial family and are naturally nocturnal. They have loose skin tissue that connects their front and hind legs, this membrane allows them to glide seamlessly through the air, just like a flying squirrel. My sugar glider will glide from across the room to me when I call his name. As owners, you should expect to spend a lot of time with your sugar glider. Typically, owning just one sugar glider is not recommended, as this may cause emotional and behavioral issues with the glider. While social companionship is crucial, the unity of multiple gliders is irreplaceable by human affection and love.

Pet stores will have pre-packaged foods that you can purchase for your glider, but they enjoy various foods, including fruits, vegetables, insects, and baby food. Large cages will allow them to hop and glide from end to end, but you also want to ensure the cage has narrow openings and is sturdy, as these critters are exceptional escape artists. They love fuzzy pockets and pouches - their cage should include at least one for them to spend their day in when they aren't awake and stimulated. They'll play with all sorts of toys for birds and rodents, such as exercise wheels, swings, or treat toys.

You can expect your glider to live 10 to 15 years, so get used to having these little guys joining your family for a while! While legal in most states, sugar gliders are not legal everywhere in the United States; in some states, it is completely illegal to own one while others allow ownership with the proper permits (such as Pennsylvania and Massachusetts). These fun bundles of love can be great pets for those willing to put in the time to care for them, but they are not for those who want a passive pet that requires low maintenance.

FERRET

IF YOU CAN GET PAST THAT MUSKY SMELL, Ferrets are great exotic companions, especially if they are handled starting at a young age! Ferrets are very playful and social animals. They love their time outside of their cage and can squeeze into just about any tight spot you can think of. Their personalities are often compared to that of cats and dogs, and they are known to be able to litter box train. However, they do need a lot of maintenance, attention, and supervision.

Ferrets have scent glands which are typically removed when they are young to get rid of their musky smell. Although, the lingering musky smell they produce can still be a problem for some with sensitive noses.

These fuzzy mischievous rodents shed a decent amount of hair and can often get hairballs. It is recommended to take them to a veterinarian annually, in order to vaccinate and prevent them from getting some of the various common health problems they might have in their lifetime.

Although they are legal in many states, make sure you observe local laws when adopting a Ferret. For example, they are banned in California, Hawaii, and New York.

HEDGEHOG

HEDGEHOGS ARE OFTEN TIMID, NOCTURNAL animals that can make great exotic pets, if lawful to own one in the state you live in. They have 7,000 quills throughout their back, and when threatened, hedgehogs will draw those quills upright and roll themselves up into a ball. They are solitary and do not like living with other hedgehogs, so you should feel comfortable adopting just one.

You will need to provide them with a spacious cage, roughly four feet long, with areas to hide, an exercise wheel, and a space heater. Hedgehogs generally get along well with other pets and are considered low maintenance companions. A hearty insect diet will allow them to live out their expectancy of four to six years. Loud noises or bright environments will stress them out, so you will want to be mindful of those when your hedgehog is out and about. Overall, hedgehogs are affordable, do not demand too much time or maintenance, and can be the perfect fit for many exotic pet seekers.

4

FENNEC FOX

As active, clever, and playful as dogs, foxes are a great companion to domesticate. As of now, certain breeds of foxes are known to be legal in fifteen U.S. states. The small, adorable, and fairly docile Fennec foxes are the most popular among exotic pet owners. It's important to keep in mind they are nocturnal (active at night), startled easily, independent, and can be territorial (if males aren't neutered). They can also get defensive if they feel threatened. Additionally, they are not the best fit for you if you prefer a quiet animal in your household, as they can be very loud with their various vocalizations.

But Fennecs can be domesticated and adapt to their owner's schedule instead of staying nocturnal, and can train to be walked on a leash. They are very active animals in the wild and require a lot of exercise.

A price under $2000 for your young Fennec fox is a red flag. It is best to acquire your Fennec fox in person from a reputable breeder. Owning a Fennec fox varies across the United States. In some areas, they are completely banned, and in others, a permit is necessary. Double-check your local laws and regulations before committing to this exotic companion.

5

SERVAL

THIS BEAUTIFUL ANIMAL IS A WILD CAT THAT
many people adopt as an exotic pet. Serval cats typically bond for life with a single human, especially if
they are hand fed and bottle raised. They are shy and
cautious of strangers but can be very affectionate and
playful. Like domestic cats, they can be litterbox

trained, but they need a gentle hand and a lot of patience to tame. They are nocturnal, active felines that need a spacious outdoor area to roam.

The diet of a Serval cat is very specific and usually consists of a whole prey protein. Frequent veterinarian visits are needed to ensure a healthy and happy Serval cat.

Serval cats are wild by nature and need a responsible owner who is skilled enough to meet the demands of the exotic feline. They are legal in 18 U.S. states, and you can acquire a Serval in North Carolina, Nevada, Wisconsin, West Virginia, Nevada, South Carolina, Alabama, and Idaho, without getting a license. In order to acquire one, you have to meet specific outdoor and environmental requirements. And without proper permits, inspections, and licenses, owning a Serval cat can be illegal, especially in Maine, Indiana, Mississippi, Texas, South Dakota, Montana, Pennsylvania, Missouri, Arizona, Oklahoma, and North Dakota. In every other state, it is illegal to own.

6
WALLABY

IT DOESN'T GET MORE EXOTIC THAN THIS.
Wallabies, indigenous to Australia, are the more
petite cousin to the Kangaroo and could be a great
exotic pet in the proper household. Their tempera-

ment varies; some are friendly and obedient, while others are frisky and anxious. Generally, they are social, cuddly, get along with other calm pets, and can accompany you around the house. They require spacious areas to roam, a warm place to retreat, and enjoy a hearty meal for their herbivore diets.

The average Bennetts Wallaby can grow to be three feet in height and weigh up to sixty pounds (females are usually smaller in size than males). Their life expectancy is generally between twelve and seventeen years.

If you are curious about owning these bouncy companions, keep in mind they can be costly. Look into local state laws and special licensing. Usually, they require specific living requirements, registration and documentation, and record-keeping. The newborn wallabies require being humanely and safely weaned from their mothers. It is ideal to speak to a veterinarian specializing in exotic animals or a reputable breeder before considering the Wallaby.

7

ANTEATER

Do you have an ant problem? Calling the exterminator might be a smart move, but before you pick up that phone, you might want to consider adopting an anteater. Famous artist, Salvador Dali, was an anteater enthusiast and has been known for sporting this fancy pet throughout Europe. There are many exotic pet lovers around the world who can't get enough of these beloved creatures.

You can find them anywhere between $5,000-$8,000. Giant Anteaters can grow up to 7 feet and be around 130 pounds. Other common species include the smaller Pygmy Anteater (fourteen inches in length), and the Northern and Southern Tamandua (four feet in length and about 10 pounds). Their life expectancy is about seven years.

Within their elongated pointy necks and snouts is an even more stretched out tongue, which is used for what anteaters are known best, enjoying some delicious termites and ants. Their tongue is very sticky and can jerk onto their potential meal at one hundred fifty times per minute.

Exotic pet owners have said Anteaters can be extremely adorable pets and can be as playful and loving as dogs. They can respond to their names being called and usually seek attention when they feel neglected.

Although, they do have a dangerous side and can use their mighty claws to defend themselves if they are threatened, making your ant problem the least of your worries. As another form of defense, they can spray a scent from their anal glands that can be quite the nose holder. Many exotic pet owners adopt hand-raised young anteaters who have grown to feel comfortable with humans. Although there are no federal laws that forbid Anteaters, certain laws within each state dictate importing, selling, and owning these exotic animals.

8

TIGER

Tigers are fierce, ferocious predators that
are not domesticated and should not be kept as pets.
Many states have instituted bans on keeping tigers as
pets, but it is legal in eight states currently. Roughly
half of all severe or fatal cat attacks are by tigers each

year, resulting in 130 maulings annually. Tigers are dangerous and unpredictable.

A cub costs around $7,500, but they'll also need an enclosure to properly house them, costing up to $20,000. They need acres of sanctuary that allows them to run, jump and roam, and it must be filled with a lot of large toys to keep these curious cats entertained. Otherwise, they can become medically depressed. A tiger's diet isn't cheap to maintain either, as they may consume nearly 90 pounds of meat in one feeding. Despite strong recommendations across the board against owning one, it is definitely one of the most exotic and flashy pets you can have!

MINIATURE DONKEY

Miniature donkeys are extremely affectionate and do great with the family. They recognize their owners and are extremely interactive and can even learn tricks. While most owners keep them as livestock, some keep them in the house as a replacement for dogs. Regardless, you will need at least a half-acre of land for them to roam free.

They can live up to forty years, so if you are considering a miniature donkey, be prepared to commit for life. They are hearty but will need care for maintaining their hooves. Miniature donkeys are relatively affordable compared to other exotic pets, ranging from $500 to $2,000. Given the right circumstances, miniature donkeys can be the perfect fit for an exotic pet seeker!

TARANTULA

I<small>F ARACHNOPHOBIA DOESN'T KEEP YOU UP AT</small> night, then a tarantula might be the right exotic pet for you. While these creepy crawlers are not the classic family pet, many intrepid arachnophiles will challenge that notion and say these warm and fuzzy spiders are great companions. They take up little

21

space, are quiet, and easy to maintain, with their favorite meals usually consisting of insects, like cockroaches, worms, and crickets.

There are about one thousand species of tarantulas, the majority of which are venomous. Although most often docile, if threatened, they will bite. Often, their venom's toxicity is like that of a wasp or a bee, but some bites can make you feel very sick and even be fatal.

The lifespan of a tarantula can vary from two to twenty years. Although you should look out for specific local laws before considering one, they are perfectly legal in many states. They can cost roughly $25 - $75. Before purchasing, test their alertness and acquire information about their age, gender, and health history; be sure you aren't getting a tarantula that might be sick or pregnant.

11

OCTOPUS

One pet, eight legs! Octopuses are the ultimate escape artists - they require extreme attention, both during setup and feeding. They are easy to feed as they will eat shrimp or clam that you can buy at any local fish store. The setup for an octopus isn't much different than any salt-water aquarium with a couple of exceptions. Firstly, octopuses live in deep waters, so the tank will need to be darker than usual. You will also want to install an oxygen filter, as many species require additional oxygen than what a typical aquarium supplies. They vary greatly in size, so the aquarium size requirement will depend on the octopus you get.

They are known to recognize their owners and are highly intelligent. As an owner, you can take them out of the water to play and keep them stimulated. Of course, you want to avoid touching your octopus if they are poisonous. Octopuses also have a beak, but do not tend to bite very often; their bite is mild. Also, beware of the ink! You'll need to manage to carefully place the octopus back in the water after being removed as they are known to release their ink once they are placed back into their home. One downside is that they do not live very long. This will also depend on the specific type of octopus, but most species will live between six months to one year in captivity.

ALPACA & LLAMA

A GROWING COMMUNITY OF LLAMA AND ALPACA lovers keep these giant fluffy creatures as pets. Alpacas come from South America and are typically larger than llamas.

You can keep llamas and alpacas together, and you should have at least three of these herd animals to ensure optimal health and happiness. The two breeds are very closely related and can live in harmony. The herd of alpaca and/or llama you get must all be the same gender due to breeding habits. You should never purchase these animals as babies as it is critical for their development to be raised by their mothers for eight to twelve months.

Their fluffy coats will need to be shaved once a year to prevent heat strokes. It is easy to house these animals as long as you have ample space for them; however, you will need to make sure predators such as dogs, wolves, and coyotes are not able to get to their area. They use a communal restroom, and you can train them to go wherever is most convenient for you. Grass and hay make up the vast majority of their diet and should always be available for them. Most cost between $3,000 to $10,000 and are legal in the vast majority of U.S. states. These fluff monsters love a caring owner and can be an outstanding choice for an exotic pet.

13

SKUNK

THE THOUGHT OF OWNING A SKUNK BRINGS UP
one big question - what about the odor?! It is legal to
de-scent these exotic pets in the United States,
which involves a surgical procedure that removes the
scent gland from your pet skunk. Skunks live 7 to 10
years and are legal to own as exotic pets in some

states; however, you will often need a permit to own one.

They are excellent climbers and diggers and are not loyal to their homes, so owners will need to have a safe and secure enclosure that is full-proof for their pets. Skunks have omnivorous diets that consist of invertebrates, fruits, and vegetables. Their long nails will need to be trimmed often and carefully. While skunks can be domesticated, they are not domesticated animals and may not be very welcoming to your hugs and cuddles. As nocturnal species, they will sleep during the day. Despite their polarizing nature, skunks can make for a unique exotic pet if sheltered and maintained properly.

14

PORCUPINE

INDEED, YOU CAN HAVE A PORCUPINE AS A PET! They are very mellow, but also prickly. So, having one of these spiky rodents requires a lot of skill and patience. They have what are called 'quills,' which are their protective spiky mechanism. I'm going to bust the myth now, they cannot shoot their quills out like darts, but with about thirty-thousand quills all over their body, they can drive 100 quills into their predator. Although they can be aggressive if they feel threatened, they can be affectionate towards humans and even trained. If you handle them properly and with care and love, you can avoid ever being pricked by them.

I'm not going to beat around the bush, porcupines need very specific care requirements and can be a big commitment. Whatever the case may be, it is important to feed these little herbivores well, because a starving porcupine is an irritated one. You should always take caution around this rodent and other animals in the house as well, the quills can be very harmful and, in some scenarios, life-threatening.

In various U.S. states having a porcupine is illegal, for example, California. Although in states like Utah and New York, they are legal. Check local laws to see if Porcupines are acquirable in your area.

SLOTH

Known for their slow movement and ultra-cute appearance, two-toed sloths can be great exotic pets for those who are willing to recreate and maintain a rainforest-like environment but want to have an exotic pet that requires little social responsibility. However, it will not be easy to provide them with an adequate environment to live in.

Sloths are arboreal creatures native to the rainforests of Central and Southern America. To recreate their environment, you will need to keep their room 80-90 degrees Fahrenheit with 80-90% humidity. They will need branches to climb and hang on. With a healthy diet of lettuce, carrots, sweet potatoes and dandelion greens, sloths can live up to thirty years. As pets, they do not like being bathed, groomed, or petted, so you will want to appreciate these majestic creatures from afar. They have long claws that they climb with, but they will rarely use their claws to attack. Sloths are priced in the range of $7,000 to $11,000.

CAPUCHIN MONKEY

OWNERS OF CAPUCHIN MONKEYS OFTEN describe the experience as taking care of an intelligent toddler that never grows up. They will require constant companionship and attention throughout the day, although they typically sleep through the night. They love to climb everything and hide their favorite toys. In addition to being highly trainable, you can work to communicate with these intelligent creatures through basic signing signals.

You will need a large cage to let them swing and play, although owners often let their pet monkeys roam through the house as well. Their diet consists of food pellets along with fruits, vegetables and baby food. If raised well, they will not bite, despite their strong canine teeth. Owning a capuchin is a remarkable experience that can be very rewarding for someone who has the time, attention, and resources to dedicate to their exotic pet.

17

CAPYBARA

As the largest rodent native to South America, the Capybara can weigh up to 110 pounds. It does have special needs that potential owners should be aware of.

The Capybara has teeth that constantly grow, so they need to chew on something all the time. Capybaras have webbed feet that allow them to swim with ease - in fact, they must have somebody of water to swim in when housed. They cannot live alone, so if you're considering adopting one, you should really be looking into adopting one more! You can train them to use a litter box and need a shady place to swim. It is legal to own these exotic pets in most states with the proper exotic pet permits.

18

BEARDED DRAGON

Bearded dragons make for great starter
pets. They are relatively easy to take care of and
require much less maintenance than many other
exotic pets on this list. Their diet consists of insects,
such as crickets and mealworms, leafy greens, and

fruit. These Australian native reptiles are easy to tame and are social with their human companions.

To house a dragon, you will need a 50 to 60-gallon aquarium and a heat source, either through a heat lamp or a ceramic heater. Additionally, ultraviolet light is critical for bearded dragons, but these bulbs are easy to obtain online or at local pet stores.

Bearded dragons have unique and fun behaviors you'll witness first-hand as a pet owner. Some of these include waving their arms to indicate submissiveness, bobbing their heads to signify dominance, puffing their spiny beard if they feel threatened, changing their skin color to display emotion, and running up the glass of the aquarium when they are bored or stressed. I know what you are thinking next - and no - they, unfortunately, do not breathe fire. If you ever thought you wouldn't be able to bond with a reptile, this friendly dragon is ready to prove you wrong!

19

MACAW

You don't need a pirate patch to have an exotic parrot on your shoulder! Macaws are legal in every state and can make wonderful pets if you have the time, care, and space to house them. There are dozens of species of macaws, varying mostly in color and size. The most common Macaw species are Scarlett, Blue and Gold, Green-wing, and Military.

Their diet consists of pelleted foods, nuts, seeds, fruits, and vegetables. As most species range from two to three-and-a-half feet tall, you will need to provide them with a cage that is at least three feet long, four feet wide, and five feet tall. The cage should be made of durable material, such as stainless steel or wrought iron, to withstand the mighty beak pressure of a macaw.

If you are looking into a pet macaw, please first witness how loud they get in person first. They are loud and they are noisy. If that may be an issue, then you should pass on this pet; however, if you can deal with that, then you can enjoy the benefits of an active and playful companion with a macaw. You can train macaws to be very friendly and interactive pets. They are considered to be one of the most intelligent species of birds and the best talking parrots. The larger the species, the longer their life expectancy, but you can expect these colorful creatures to live 30-50 years.

CHINCHILLA

THIS EXOTIC PET TAKES THE AWARD FOR THE softest fur. Chinchillas are a great pet to have but need a lot of maintenance and patience. They are very energetic, playful, and nocturnal. If properly handled when young, they can form a close bond and be tamed by their owners. Although they don't enjoy cuddling or being held like other domestic animals, they can often show affection in various other ways.

Chinchillas prefer specific routines and require spacious cages for exercise and play. Be very cautious of warm temperatures as their hefty fur can cause them to overheat. They require a specific diet and a special bath called a "Dust Bath" if you want to keep their fur soft and thick. Contrary to human baths, these Chinchilla baths are vigorous and contain special dust which helps clean their fur and keep it in pristine condition.

You can generally purchase these luxurious rodents at a pet store or a breeder. Both males and females have a similar life expectancy of about fifteen to twenty-two years, and range from 10-14 inches in length (not counting their tails).

BALL PYTHON

Ball Pythons are slow-moving snakes that do not tend to be aggressive. You can have a relaxing relationship with these snakes as they have very calm demeanors; however, as babies, they may be a bit more tense and nippy. Pythons come in a large variety of colors and morphs for you to choose, although some morphs will have health issues due to how they are bred.

In general, they will eat once a week. It is common for ball pythons to be picky and particular eaters - some will only eat if the temperature is right, some will only eat live food, and others will simply be on an unknown feeding strike. Frozen feed is the best option for this snake in order to prevent disease transfer from live feed, and you can typically find frozen feed at your local pet store. You should provide ball pythons with at least a 70-gallon tank so they can stretch out their four to six feet bodies if they desire. This species is considered the best pet reptile while awarding its owner with an exotic pet owner's title.

LEAVE A 1-CLICK REVIEW!

I would be incredibly thankful if you could take just 60 seconds to write a brief review on Amazon, even if it's just a couple sentences!

SCAN QR CODE ABOVE OR CLICK LINK BELOW:
https://www.amazon.com/review/create-review/?&
asin=Bo8RJ2YGFL

CONCLUSION

Exotic pets are available everywhere around the U.S. in one form or another, but there is often more effort required to be an exotic pet owner than might meet the eye. Before embracing such a lifestyle, make sure you have what it takes to adopt the species you are interested in. We often adopt an animal because it brings us joy, laughter, and happiness. Our responsibility is to ensure the feeling is reciprocated with the unlikely companions we bring to our families. Many animal rights advocates are against captivating exotic animals. They make a good point; the last thing you want is for an irresponsible person to bring an amazing animal into their home and not know how to care for it, causing the animal to suffer or pass away. That's why it is important to do your research and be fully prepared because, at the end of the day, the animal's life and well-being are in your hands.

Also, some areas allow pet kangaroos or squirrels, while others might have banned rabbits as pets. You must consult your local and state laws to check that the exotic pal you are seeking is legal in your area, especially because these restrictions are constantly changing. You will also want to find a veterinarian who is able and willing to see your new friend. These are just some of the first steps I would recommend before making the move to adopt. Watch plenty of videos, join a Facebook group with owners, and thoroughly research the specific breed you are interested in..

I am rooting for you! If you are able to overcome the barriers, the benefits of owning an exotic pet are remarkable. You will experience a unique relationship between a human and another species. Your friends will be intrigued, and you will have a companion to brag about, with endless eccentric stories. It won't be easy, but the rewards are endless!

17 Cutest Baby Animals you wouldn't believe...

This booklet includes:

- 17 OF THE MOST ADORABLE BABY ANIMALS THAT WILL BRING A SMILE TO YOUR FACE
- SURPRISING FUN FACTS ABOUT THESE ANIMALS THAT YOU NEVER KNEW

Get this free booklet and share the fun with these adorable animals that will make your day!

To receive your free _Cutest Baby Animals_ booklet, click the link or scan the QR code below:

https://purelypublishing.activehosted.com/f/7

REFERENCES

8 Best Large Talking Pet Parrots. (n.d.). The Spruce Pets. Retrieved 2020, from https://www. thesprucepets.com/large-parrots-that-can-talk-390522

A Guide to Caring for Bearded Dragons as Pets. (n.d.). The Spruce Pets. Retrieved September 20, 2020, from https://www.thesprucepets.com/ bearded-dragons-as-pets-1236896

All About Sugar Gliders. (2017, December 22). Petmd.Com. https://www.petmd.com/exotic/care/ all-about-sugar-gliders

Caring for a Serval Cat as an Exotic Pet. (n.d.). The Spruce Pets. Retrieved 2020, from https://www. thesprucepets.com/serval-cats-1238152

Do Wallabies Make Good Pets? (n.d.). The Spruce Pets. Retrieved 2020, from https://www. thesprucepets.com/pet-wallabies-1238323

Hedgehog Pets Cute But Challenging - Veterinary Medicine at Illinois. (n.d.). University of Illinois

College of Veterinary Medicine. Retrieved 2020, from https://vetmed.illinois.edu/pet_column/hedgehog-pets/

How to Take Care of Pet Tigers. (n.d.). The Spruce Pets. Retrieved September 20, 2020, from https://www.thesprucepets.com/pet-tigers-1238150#:%7E:text=Tigers%20are%20not%20domesticated%20cats.&text=Tigers%20are%20huge%2C%20strong%2C%20fanged,as%20pets%20at%20any%20age.

Keeping and Caring for Fennec Foxes as Pets. (n.d.). The Spruce Pets. Retrieved 2020, from https://www.thesprucepets.com/about-fennec-foxes-as-pets-1236778

Keeping and Caring for Tarantulas as Pets. (n.d.). The Spruce Pets. Retrieved September 20, 2020, from https://www.thesprucepets.com/pet-tarantulas-1237346

Learn How to Take Care of a Pet Chinchilla. (n.d.). The Spruce Pets. Retrieved 2020, from https://www.thesprucepets.com/chinchillas-1236769

Make Sure Your Home is Safe for Your Ferret. (n.d.). The Spruce Pets. Retrieved 2020, from https://

www.thesprucepets.com/ferret-proofing-your-home-1238653

Randall-Texas A&Amp;M, K. (2013, May 9). *Genome shows macaw is one smart bird.* Futurity. https://www.futurity.org/genome-shows-macaw-is-one-smart-bird/#:%7E:text=%E2%80%9CThey%20are%20considered%20to%20be,a%20wingspan%20approaching%20four%20feet

Solomon, K. (2019, October 3). *14 animals that are surprisingly legal to own as pets in the US.* Business Insider Nederland. https://www.businessinsider.nl/animals-legal-pets-us-surprising-2019-10?international=true&r=US

Use This Guide to Care for Macaws. (2018). The Spruce Pets. https://www.thesprucepets.com/macaws-1239204#:%7E:text=A%20well%2Dcared%2Dfor%20macaw,also%20make%20them%20chal-lenging%20pets.

What Is Your Bearded Dragon Trying to Tell You? (n.d.). The Spruce Pets. Retrieved 2020, from https://www.thesprucepets.com/bearded-dragon-behaviors-1238400

Made in the USA
Columbia, SC
06 December 2024

48180925R00040